DAN BRODNITZ

The Lavender Lemonade Is Back

Poems and Stories

Long Sky Media

Copyright © 2020 by Dan Brodnitz
All rights reserved.

No part of this book may be reproduced or used in any format or by any means, electronic or mechanical, including photocopying, recording, scanning, or by any information storage and retrieval device or system, without prior written permission from the publisher.

Published in the United States by Long Sky Media, sending out signals from the island city of Alameda, California.

Find us online: LongSkyMedia.com

ISBN: 978-1-946588-02-9

Some of these poems and stories appeared previously in books and magazines, including *Coffeehouse, ProgressChrome, Red Hills Review, Snow Monkey, Two Bridges, Shampoo,* and *Work.* Many thanks!

Cover design by Helen Bruno

Book design by Tony Jonick

Illustrations by Arthur Johnstone

Back cover bio photo by Gerhard Koren

Printed in the United States of America

To Barbara, Susannah, and Sam

Very big thanks to Julia Park Tracey, George Guida, and Susannah Brodnitz for reading poems and prose and helping pick the ones that made the cut. To Rodney Koeneke for early kind words that meant more than he likely realized. To Elisabeth Beller, Tony Jonick, and Helen Bruno—true friends and publishing pros all!

Thanks to Gerhard Koren for a lovely photo taken on a cold day. And to Artie Johnstone for his wonderful illustrations and cover art.

Contents

Eggs and Feathers 1
Bean Song 2
Circus Ghosts 3
Everyday Chug 4
Forget Not the Mud 5
He's a Truck 6
My Unkind Moment 7
This Poem Is with Stupid 8
Flea Market Fandango, 1985 9
Skin 10
End Times 11
Emoticon Rescue 12
Those Nails 13
Legends from My Childhood #1: Melancholy Mom 14
75/25 15
Gathering My Stones 16
Among My Souvenirs 17
Old Dude Goes to a Show 18
First, the Flash 19
Unphotographed Pets 20
I Want to Build a House 21
Zombie Adventures, Please 22
Wire Act 23

Bedtime	24
Conversation	25
Woosh	26
Strom	27
Tucker Carlson	28
It's Me	29
Always Starting	30
Ta Da	31
Were They Bats?	32
Uh Oh	33
Myth of Bone	34
Cat-Pinned	35
Kiss	36
Welcome	37
Legends from My Childhood #4: The Showman	38
Morning Lion	39
Family Lore	40
Living in Ruins	42
Long Gone	43
He's Breaking All the Time	44
Great-Grandfather's Beard	45
Happy Water	46
You, Triumphing at Last, Flags Wave	47
I'll Draw the Hair	48
Morning Sounds	49
Righteous, Stressed-Out Daddy-o	50

Lift	51
The Lavender Lemonade Is Back	52
"You want a piece of me, chair?"	53
Crispy Yum Yum Child of God	54
Clean	55
Flamingo Discard	56
Quiet and Comfortable	57
Not a Snake	58
The New Ralph Macchio	59
Wall Pile	60
Call the Water	61
Escobar's Cold	62
Graze	63
The Getaway	64
Just FYI	66
Looking Back	67
Sanity	68
In Florida	69
Smaller, Slender, Grave	70
Shaved My Beard	71
No One Should Suffer	72
The Pencil They Gave Me	73
Soul	74
Espresso Poems	75
The Perfect Gentleman	76

The Lavender Lemonade
Is Back

Poems and Stories

Eggs and Feathers

I'll admit that I was a little surprised this past weekend by the flurry of emails I received in response to the (arguably tepid) stand I took against eggs and feathers. Or rather, against the "egg and feather" craze that's been blighting hipster shacks like "Zack's Breakfastery" in Detroit and "The Most Important Meal" in Kansas City.

Josh from Hoboken writes: "Dear Dan: you are a big jerk. Eggs and feathers wrawk! Stop saying bad things about eggs and feathers!"

Doug in Chicago writes: "Mr. Brodnix (sic): you and everyone else over the age of twenty-five can eat your eggs the way you like. I'll have mine with feathers!"

Perhaps the authors of these misbegotten missives think I can be scared into silence. If anything, the result has been the obverse. With each new addled assault that stumbles its way into my inbox, I find myself emboldened to take up the battle cry against this repulsive phenomenon with plus vigor ("more vigor")!

Dishes like "Eggs Benedict (and Feathers)" or "Eggs Over Medium (and Feathers)" or even "(Feathers and) Soft Boiled Egg" are just the latest step in la grande decline ("the grand decline"). And I for one will not sit quietly by, tuning my viola while Rome cooks egg dishes decorated with feathers!

Bean Song

Counting beans, one for every
word you said today.

A waterfall of frozen
lima bean conversation.

Bright bean rage.
Soft, velvety heirloom beans.

Bean opera. Beans buzzing
in a thick glass jar.

Where do all these beans come from?—
these beans, with no apologies.

And why is it that you find yourself
at this late stage

so full of frigging
beans?

Circus Ghosts

Most people don't like ghosts.
But everybody loves circus ghosts.

Circus ghosts may not remember
who they were in the real world or
what kind of car they drove.

But they remember their tricks.

They say: "Watch me juggle. I can eat fire."

"oooOOOOOoooo."

"I can eat fire."

Everyday Chug

Everybody's tired of it today.
Tired of the same old everyday vibrations
chugging through their bodies
down from their throats to
their hands
to the ground.

The lechers are too tired to lech today.
You see?

Dogs don't even try to lick their buddies.

The sidewalk prophets are even putting down their
signs, even walking off their jobs
saying: "Doom.
Whatever.
Doom."

Forget Not the Mud

Forget not the mud-caked juice box,
those traces of familiar sweetness locked in
Hannukah gelt coin coverings dented
dirtward
next to
a plate or two of shaded eggplant parmigiana.

There was a party here.

There were frightened
earthworms. Thunder above. Gray light. And children being
irresponsible.

He's a Truck

A red-cabbed rig
flying just above the spires of Golden Gate Bridge.
What the hell—right? A truck, aloft? Sort of lovely
though for the moment, looking around. There's
a nice stereo and tapes and a bed tucked in
behind the driver's seat.
The problem's his trajectory.
He'd hoped he might line up
with the road below, touch down, head on over to
Sausalito for a movie. But there's too much
sideways momentum and the truck flew west.
Flew past. Drifted.
Over. Out.

My Unkind Moment

He looked like he was drawn
not with a pen or a paintbrush
but with the dull wet end of a used toothpick.

A dent. An imprint.
A soft image.

Leaving behind
a flaw designed primarily
to gather dust.

This Poem Is with Stupid

We were so lucky
to be kids
right there
in the sticky sweet center of
the golden age
of t-shirts.

Mall-store walls plastered to the sky
with receding rows of iron-ons.
And when one of my older brothers
wore that shirt with the frog on it that said:
"I'm so happy I could just shit,"
Well I was that happy too.

Flea Market Fandango, 1985

Bladed stars
shuriken with bright black tips
spread out wide against soft cassis cardboard like bats
behind a glass case.

I'm shopping from a safe distance.
Five feet back, where the merchant
can't catch my breath.

Ten minutes or so and
now my sneakers have set
into the tire treads of this rained out road.

The morning's bagel keeps me warm.
I'm not shopping really.
Just standing still.

Bladed stars, grant me ninja speed.
Focus.
Precision.

Skin

He had two
tattoos
when they got married

But then it turned out
she didn't like
tattoos

So he got another
and another.

Until she left him alone
with his skin.

End Times

"When the Fish People come," the General said, "you'll want to have ice nearby. Lots of it. In this heat, the Fish People can overpower you like *that!*" He snapped his fingers.

Suzie scribbled a quick note in her pad and circled it:

"Ice."

* * *

"When you get to Earth, start decomposing right away," David Fish-People told his class. "Your smell will reduce their ability to resist. The sooner you start to decompose, the easier it'll be on our troops."

The students nodded, and Daphne FishPeople spoke quietly into her digital recorder:

"Decompose."

Emoticon Rescue

It's the smiley that really breaks my heart
the little happy face you
tack on
right after you break goodbye, say the news, share that thing.

You're happy. And I'm glad for it.
But where is your nose?

Now who will save
your missing nose?

Those Nails

Pity poor Pol Pot's cat.
Hitler's hamster.

Fed by this thing.
Stroked by this thing.

By this skin
those nails
they scratch
that spot.

Pity poor Pol Pot's cat.

Legends from My Childhood #1: Melancholy Mom

She took too many pills or something
and nearly died
but the main thing I remember
is sitting down at their
kitchen table and her
telling us how at that critical moment
she saw the light and turned back.

I thought: "She seems sad."
And: "I can't believe a grownup is
telling me this and treating me
like I'm a grownup
when I'm not."

On Halloween, she dressed me
up as a '50s kid and put my hair
in a DA with goop.

She told me that the look worked—
that I had a '50s face. And I
took that as a
compliment.

75/25

"It's a multiple of a lot of different things."
Then somewhere down the line, you find yourself saying
"It's a syndrome."

You're giving 75/25. Or 65/35.
You're holding back.

Not out of laziness but from some sense
that things are finite and you don't want to spend it all.

When the phone rings, you answer it on the fourth ring.
Or you go to an adult valentine-making class
and you say: "Nice to meet you."
But you don't make enough valentines for everyone. Just two or three.

Your basketball buddies don't even bring it up.
The way you've stopped saying
"*That's* what I'm *talking* about" with your trademark vigor.

So you head out to a farm or a petting zoo,
someplace with a gate and a quarter twist
for food in hand
because animals can't tell the difference.

Except that maybe you're easier to sit on nowadays.
That goat is so heavy.
Come on now, you big old goat.

Move.

Gathering My Stones

Other boys stay out late and smoke.
They use bad words.
They worship false gods.

When they ask me to come along, I say I'm busy.

I'm keeping my hands clean.
It's been hard work, really really hard work
keeping my hands clean
all these years.

I do not live in a glass house.
I am not one of those people.
I've earned the right.

And now I'm throwing rocks at you.

Among My Souvenirs
Adapted from a tale told by my grandfather, Irving Feinerman

Well, my mother went into a shoemaker
with an old pair of shoes.

He opened up the bottom.
Nailed in the 15 dollars for the transit across the river.

And the women were put on a wagon.
And the men were driven on by foot.
Walking in pitch darkness.

You know the song.

I was almost half frozen there in the ravine.
And I realized it may not be a safe thing to have
so close to the five-pointed Red Army star.

So as I was sitting there on the ground
sharpening with the dust
I buried it there.

I was born in a small town in the Ukraine.
We were afraid to move even to the next town.

I celebrated my 17th birthday in Bucharest on April 15th.
That was just about a month before we came to the United States.

This is the saga of my coming to the United States.

It's a long story.

Old Dude Goes to a Show

Five minutes after the lights go down
I hear a familiar rustling two seats over.
Someone's making things happen.

I'm a little stressed but not surprised
when a hand in the darkness offers
two white pills.

"No thanks," I say, false cool, thinking:
"I am old dude."

The hand withdraws.

A minute later, I ask:
"What was that? 'E'? Ecstasy?"

"Altoids."

And I nod a short,
tight nod,
as if that was my second guess.

First, the Flash

on the plane ride home
that I might be the one who dies young—
that flimsy-bodied office worker whose organs
give out.

Then the round
retired banker capturing me at the local tea shop
telling me only the rich are happy

that I don't really know Orange County.
That I'm due for a double-chinned heart attack
and what will happen to my wife and kids then?

Finally a voicemail from my doctor saying
hi
my total cholesterol is high
I'm at high risk for cardiac disease.

She hopes it's OK to leave this in a message
but she's going on vacation.

And it comes roaring out
like some kind of pressure-cooked stew where you
can't make out the specific vegetables involved
but it's obvious something's
been mashed.

Unphotographed Pets

Held with small hands
cupped and callous-free

sometimes lose their names
change color over time

as six dead gerbils shade
to four black mice

and goldfish replicate.
Was it two turtles? Or a bird
on my shoulder?

I Want to Build a House

I want to build a house with
Richard Brautigan
up on the third floor.

Looking out a large window
at open land, hands
on the windowsill.

Wearing that old hat
that old vest

those old glasses.

He looks good.

Zombie Adventures, Please

I will eat pizza and oversized subs and drink soda.
We'll tear stretch rubber masks off
cranky senior delinquents.

> *They have their complaints.*
> *I have complaints too.*
> *You don't see me acting out.*

Snoopy and Scoob will tug and growl
over a torn blanket.

The girls will help me fold my
zig-zag t-shirt at night.
Read me stories as I
lay my large round head
down to rest.

Release me from this dustbowl, Fred. From this house.
This baseball field. These shrill harpies.

Let me ride along
in your stinky van.

Wire Act

We saw this squirrel the other night. And she's carrying one of her kids in her mouth over a thin black power line—tree to tree, in search of better digs.

In her mouth! POWER line! Or... maybe it was a telephone line. But either way, it was crazy.

So she drops the first kid off on a big branch, takes a quick breath, and then heads back out to get kid number two.

This time across, she seems wiped out, stumbling dramatically—we gasp! This is thirty feet over the concrete sidewalk. And kid number two is huge. At least half its mother's size.

Well the mom just barely makes it over, but make it over she does. We all cheer! And then back she goes. Step, step, then lying down on the wire, lying down. Embracing that wire, then step, step, oh god I'm so beat stumble. Lie down. Again. Then step. Spent.

We wonder why she doesn't just walk on the sidewalk, nudging them along with her nose? A thin wire? Thirty feet in the air? Why make it so hard? And then we realized Oh yeah. For a squirrel it's like: "We die on the ground."

Bedtime

She slept in the bed
while he slept on the couch
so he could hear their sick daughter
and her three-day-old cough.

And in the morning
while she moved around the kitchen
and the kids watched too-loud TV
and coughed a little more,

he crept back into the bed,
curled up in the body warmth
she'd left behind

and they slept together
separated
only by time.

Conversation

I'm the kind of husband
who starts talking to his wife
before entering the house,
while the door is still closed,
through the open peephole.

And she's the kind of
wife who answers
before I find my keys.

Woosh

That's the goal. To open it
one more crack.
Bathe in the woosh.
Fire it back.
Not to be Superman.
But to stick our heads
into the place
where the idea of Superman came from
and then wriggle out
trout
in teeth.

Strom

Senator Strom Thurmond belongs to my gym.
I see him there three, four times a week.
On the treadmill.
Sculpting his biceps.
His rock hard abs.
He doesn't listen to music while he works out.
He just stares straight ahead
with his iron skull and his
wide, bony eye sockets.
I try to tell him it's overkill.
"Senator, really.
At your advanced age
one time a week
would be more than enough."
He snarls at me. "Son," he says.
"You don't know shit."

Tucker Carlson

How many times must I not
watch you how many channels
do I need to chase you away from
before you get the point?

If I must not watch you a million times.
If I must not watch you till the solar core
inside my TV cools and its silver casing cracks

until my many remotes retreat into open palms
rush back toward some lost part of my
insides
until my eyelashes gray and wilt
and spiral off
that

will be
my pleasure.

It's Me

I saw you watching when I got up
and I want to reassure you,
it's not you, it's me. It's not the way
you were snapping your fingers. Or how
loudly you were breathing. Sure,
I don't like your shirt. But
there are lots of shirts
here I don't like.
Look at that guy, for example.

No, this is about me.
And the choices I've made.
The potatoes I had last night, for example.

Always Starting

Johnny was always starting gangs
but he rarely finished them.

Which explained all those half-formed gangs
hanging around town
looking for Johnny.
Not really sure.

What to do next.

Ta Da

He said "ta da"
because he wanted them to spot
the magic. The unicorn and its twisted horn.

The wand and its wand rainbows
all spark to celebrate
that spreadsheet.

Uh Oh

He can see
in her eyes
that she can see
in his eyes
the crazy.

Were They Bats?

Were they birds or were they bats?
Does it matter?
When they drop down in darkness.
When they brush up against the back of your head and nudge you along.
When they flap in your hair.
You want to know.
Beaks or black noses? Bony wings?
Were they bats?

Myth of Bone

Do you believe you have bone inside you?

Have you bought stock
in the scam that
you're made of stone?

Why not skin? Solid through?
Why not dense-coiled hair
to prop your fading hips?

As if we have a pelvis inside us.

Tell me this: how did that stone
get in there? That stone called
"bone"?

And how come that stone isn't worn
by time
to a pebble?

Cat-Pinned

Cat-pinned
warm butterfly
  me beneath the blanket
  with my warm beneath the blanket
    in my crook
    she's a tack
    pinned me down
till I flutter flutter
stop.
she stays warm
I can't move
she don't care.
and I stop.

Kiss

She's crying
and hacking
and they're both
clean and he's
wearing a Tiny Toons
backpack.

He gives her a kiss, small and nervous.

Like one bird
stumbling back
into another.

Welcome

Welcome
to the Golden Age
of me flossing my teeth.

An upgraded Age of Reason
and now even the common man understands

that the pale dots
on my bathroom mirror
are just pale dots and not some grim portent.

At night there is light
in this magical time.

I am guided by the soft reflection of
my polished mouth bone

and these gums
have never felt
so fierce.

Morning Lion

My two-year-old
roars at me,
a lion
up close
with orange-juice breath.

Legends from My Childhood #4:
The Showman

"They used to call me 'Gentile Joe'" he said.
'Cuz my name is 'Joe Gentle.' I loved the Jews. Oh sure.
I loved the Jews and the Jews loved me."

Pulling out tinted photos of foxy showgirls from the '30s.
"The ladies, the ladies. Oh sure."

Stacked instruments
music stands and guitar picks
dirty music sheets for sale
dog at his feet and
three 17-year-olds he was
charming us now.

We loitered and listened to old stories
put across with a lewd twinkle.

"Here, have a patch cord," he said when we moved to leave.
"Have a drum stick." I still have that drum stick.

Family Lore

We were seventeen years old and driving up to Vermont in Tom's car: Danny, Tom, Kelly, and me—Tom at the wheel.

To pass some time, we reminisced about a former friend, last name Bigelow, even dorkier than us and generally pitied; but yes, a few years before, we'd hung out with him a little, and OK, the three of us guys had all played Dungeons and Dragons at Bigelow's house more than once. No denying it, Bigelow had a Charlie Brown head.

The day was going smoothly enough. High spirits, no traffic. And then Tom dropped the bomb. His parents, nice folks: religious, thin, outdoorsy, and quiet—in the privacy of their home they had a nickname for poor Bigelow. They called him "Pumpkin Head."

And this kind of horrified Danny and me—that Tom's thin parents with their outdoorsy ways could sit in the living room, fire burning, Tom and his older brother reading religious books on the couch, Tom's parents in their favorite firm armchairs, in front of the fire, sitting fragile and tall; and then Tom's dad looks up from his fly fishing magazine and he says:

"Maw?" corn patch twang.

"Yes, Paw?" her voice, floating up river with a long, steady beat between each word.

"You know that Bigelow boy Tom plays the devil game with?"

"Yes, Paw," turning a page in last year's almanac while Tom and his brother tune in, silently anticipating.

"You ever look at his skull up close like?"

"Yes, Paw."

"I been thinkin', Hell if it don't look like a…"

"Yes, Paw?"

". . . like a PUMPkin." And Paw lets loose some shallow breathing, puppy dog pleased with himself, while Maw looks over and mock scolds him, a light slap on the knee.

Another pause. Then, "Paw?" carefully placing her book on a small oak table that sits in between them.

"Yes, Maw?"

"From now on, let's call him…" one more pause as she smiles wide, "PUMPkin Haid!" And Tom's whole family just laughs and laughs until his brother laughs himself onto the floor, gasping for air, pleading for mercy and a hand up so he can return to his spot on the couch.

Well I'm sure that's not how it happened, and, in point of fact, both his parents have network news accents or close enough, but that's how we rode Tom while he drove the car and us in it from New Jersey, through Massachusetts, all the way up to Vermont and a week with his folks at the house his family owned. His grandfather had designed that house, carefully landscaped the property—huge by New Jersey standards—to make it look like something pulled from a painting. That's what Tom would tell us. Of course, we'd have to wait a day or two before he was ready to hand out any more family lore.

As we continued to speed north, conversation in that car just slowed to a halt. Tom was understandably irritated, and I was more than a little creeped out. It was a brutal decade: adults making fun of thirteen-year-olds and Reagan in the White House.

Living in Ruins

All these East Side apartment buildings we live in
   with long, brown walls, cracked hallways veined stone,
   elevators with paint-chipped, slow closing sheet-metal doors.

All these Indiana condos
   with thin, water-stained carpets.

These Utah duplexes
   with cat-scratched screens
   and deep-gouged hardwood floors.

All these buildings
in various states of decay.

And all of us living in ruins.

Long Gone

Today my son
is the Black Fox

in a one-kid revival
of the '50s classic, *The Court Jester*

as he stands around the kitchen shouting:
"Hawkins, get out of my clothes."
"Hawkins, get out of my clothes!"

He wants to play with Danny Kaye
but Danny Kaye is long gone.

He's Breaking All the Time

"He's breaking all the time!"
our cabbie says.
He's what?

"The cab in front of me is breaking all the time!"
Oh my lord. Somebody stop him.
We need time!

And then of course I realize it's
just that it's late and I'm
skating along.

"He's braking all the time"
is all that other car's doing.
His backlights flash and flash and flash.

Our taxi scoops around, passes on the right.
Bright white bolts of drizzle slam into the road
streaming it back out behind us faster than we can parse.

All part of
that necklace I wear made of
night trips home from the airport.

Great-Grandfather's Beard

Been thinking about
my great-grandfather's beard.

I can't compete with that.

Puffy-white sketched
lawyer-still.

Coffee, ironed tablecloths, small spoons.
Not one drop swings
loose.

Cigars for all. Corona de Luxe
smoke drifts
over old Europe squares.

Sons in perfect pose. Even the camera man
had his act together.

Happy Water

My friend told
my four-year-old daughter
that she was 70 percent water.

She laughed and laughed
and clapped her hands.

I don't think I've ever
seen her more happy.

"That was fun," she said,
"what do you mean?"

You, Triumphing at Last, Flags Wave

the elephants do their dance
and you know that it's your time
how they're dancing for you
how they've painted their names
how they've polished their pokey things
and you're just sitting back and letting
the bump of their girth
flop you out of your
chair with each move
flop you out
onto the dance floor
and you're thinking

I'm dancing
and it's effortless.

Look at me.

I'll Draw the Hair

If we're all drawing a face together
I don't want to draw the mouth.

I'll draw the hair—
lines, loose and easy.

Or the eyes looking
off to
one side.

But not the lips.
The way they curve and join
and hold back
her teeth.

Don't make me draw the lips.

Morning Sounds

Twee birds, rumbling boat horns,
rough timber movement

rolled up for the night
into a living room carpet spiral
with socks and cat toys,
spoons, string, lost chopsticks.

Leaned sideways through the timeline,
bending toward a corner wall.

Then shook out
at new light.

Dropping like 6 am jacks
onto hardwood floor.

Righteous, Stressed-Out Daddy-o

"Hey Potty-Mouth!
   Like,
stop expanding
my toddler's
vocabulary."

shouts my inner, angry
uptight beatnik
to this guy sitting two rows back.

And I toss an espresso over
one shoulder into the eyes
of this small-smiling fuck.

I maim him with
my poetry.

I thunder him
with cartoon thoughts

in my inner,
angry, uptight
beatnik mind.

Lift

Up on those shoulders,
hands clutched
together in clumps of see-through white.

He walks you around the edge of the lake, smiling.
You look forward, seeing the world through his cherry tobacco hum.
You're grandpa's face today. You're giving that to him.

And he's giving you lift.

The Lavender Lemonade Is Back

The lavender lemonade is back
at my local coffee shop.
I'd given up on her.

All the lemon factories, moved off-planet.
"We Thank You For Your Business."

Empty cups, traced with
mint and cane.

I've been lost
behind the

lost

behind the
dark berry side of this Lavender Moon.

Here comes the lemonade.

"You want a piece of me, chair?"

said my five-year-old tonight, dressed in
full Batman togs, before delivering
360 degrees of pain

to the sides, the back,
the seat of our
oversized wooden rocker.

"Hunh? Chairie?" he cooed.
"You want a piece of me, Chairie?"

And somehow that familiar name
only made
the beating
more savage.

Crispy Yum Yum Child of God

The cinnamon chicken
slid off the car roof.
Gourmet exploding.
Big
  messy
    boom.
     Plate shards, scattered like shark teeth.
     Chicken shards, scattered like chicken.
     On the driveway. In the lawn.
And jeez:
    what a strange fate
    for this
    lightly basted
    cinnamon flavored
      crispy yum yum
      child of God.

Clean

Little bird people
with their hollow bones
heads uplifted

trying out afterhours fancy soap.
Bath salts.
Sugar scrubs.

Sometimes
it's not all about you

applying topical sweetness.

Sometimes
it's all about

traffic hums
warm door

happy birds.

Flamingo Discard

The whistle blew
and the teacher screamed:
"I don't see you *freezing*.
That's not *freezing*."

And the little boy froze
as best he could,

hopping a small, desperate, one-legged hop

like a discard from the Flamingo Factory,

like a Frankenstein's Monster
made from flamingo parts.

Hop... hop... hop...
slowing like your last few, tired heartbeats,
like your final, frozen breath,

and then he fell down.

Quiet and Comfortable

David lived in a small apartment. It was tidy but modest—the sort of place a young math teacher might set up. David was an old math teacher, clinging to his youth.

He had two closets, a set of World encyclopedias, a wicked (that is to say, evil) sofa that made him moan and clutch his sides whenever he sat down, and a kitchen full of unnamable appliances.

His shoes were quiet and comfortable, and his life was as empty as the set of all numbers greater than six, yet less than four. In most ways, he lived an ordinary life. But he wasn't ordinary. He was unusual. And when no one else was around he'd sit very still, and he'd prove it.

"Spotlight on seasoning!" he'd shout. "Bring on the dancing girls!"

The lights would dim, not as if by magic but by magic itself. Thin smoke would creep across the living room floor. Then, with a burble, before his eyes and to his delight, out would pop three Squatting Demons, slope-browed as you please. And they sang. And they wore tights. And they brandished electric pepper grinders that lit up when you used them so you could see how much pepper you were grinding.

"More grinding!"
he'd call.

"Bore brinding!"
they'd scream. And
the night would fade
as the pepper flew.

Not a Snake

You say I'm a snake but a snake
moves with purpose, right?

They lead with their head. Reach
with their mouth. Draw a
dry belly line with intent dotting
each turn.

Have you ever seen a snake tumble? Or trip? Or twist?

Not a snake.

The New Ralph Macchio

People have been wondering for some time now who the new Ralph Macchio will be. They say: "Who?"

Well, I have the answer, and I'm going to share it.

But I think it will come as a big surprise, so brace yourself.

I am the new Ralph Macchio.

Ralph knows already, and he's not happy about it. But so what. And maybe you're not happy either. But I'll tell you what I told him. I said: "Suck on this, Ralph."

He had his chance. It's my turn now.

It's my turn to be Ralph Macchio.

Wall Pile

Wet ride this morning.
Chalk bricks trying to absorb
pulling it in cold wood
old wood.
Paper mats.

His wet feet uncovered, yes?
Flat cats lick his feet.

Vapor socks.
Lick sneaker pump.
Lick vapor swoosh.

And those feet stir.

Now he's caressing some space saying:
"Hi. I will stab you in your leg."
Really? Well.
I don't see a knife.

Hopping past.

Hoping stone
soon dry
out.

Call the Water

Is it enough
to call the water
black to talk about
the swirls, the crack in
the floor of this Bay

That steams up
sleep evaporating
soaking into
a newspaper headline
till it has mighty heft

Is now a good time
to chalk it all up
this swirl and this crack
this slow-dripping heft

To some sort of
vague, tectonic displacement?

Some foamy kerning surge?

Escobar's Cold

Escobar couldn't hear so good.

His cold—the same cold he was
complaining about last month—
had taken root now, deep inside
the curly spots that led from ears to brain.

You might think he would open his eyes
wider to compensate, to pull in
extra visual cues.

But he was going the other way instead.

Withdrawing like evening fish.
Letting things happen around him without much fuss.

For example: when that guy flipped him off,
Pablo Escobar (1949-1993) just nodded.

Graze

The horses are grazing over at the World Trade Center.
Tourists form a wide circle around the field

translating plaques out loud to each other
looking down at the grass-covered pit

before strolling over to the local Fire Department
where the hay stacks are piled higher than feels safe.

Squinting through dark glass into the station
past the truck, past the pole

they're looking for a cow they can rope or a lunch bell to ring
in this unexpected land of big sky.

The Getaway

This weekend I dropped by to see Mr. Davis (not his real name), the ninety-four-year-old man who lives around the corner. I was interested in hearing what it was like growing up in the Oklahoma and Missouri Ozark Mountains during the 1910s and '20s. And we talked about that for a little over an hour.

When I got up to leave he started to tell me one more story—something from more recent times. As he spoke, he was sitting across from me in a room filled with things he'd made or repaired himself, useful things, most of them steel. Mr. Davis described a lady he'd met a few years back, some time after Mrs. Davis had passed away.

"Well this woman, she got to coming up by here a foot. She's older woman, kinda slim. And she stop a little bit, finally got to stoppin' out there and go in and set with me in the garden.

"She said she lived in the back part of The Getaway."

(The Getaway used to be a bar, but somewhere along the line it was turned into a house. The old sign's still out front but now there are curtains in the windows.)

"That's the only thing she told me, and I couldn't find her name or nothin' in the phone book.

"I went down there once. Drove in the side way. I didn't see no way you could go to the back of The Getaway from in there. Seemed like she said you went in this side of The Getaway. That street and in the back. In the back of The Getaway she said.

"So I went looking for a way into the back part of The Getaway building. I don't know if that's what she meant or not.

"I still don't know if that's where she lived."

Mr. Davis laughed for a moment, with his bright smile and then he went a little quiet. It was a mystery, what had happened. And he was sorting through the facts.

"She may have died by now, she was in the hospital a time or two, something wrong with her. She was about…eighty years old.

"I don't know."

He paused.

"Can't live forever, I'll tell you."

Just FYI

I am the just fy
the optional information
the only information

you do not need
to act on me.

Have no fear old friend.

No change no motion
no response
required.

Remain as you were
more or less absorb me

and roll on.

Looking Back

He described his life as a series of tasks
days filled
with the description of those tasks

how he'd cut the boards
what he did in the cotton gin
how he'd made the metal bracings
for that black chair in front of his house
that he sat in
most days.

It was like asking a chef for her life story
and she says
well,
I made my first cake when I was 8.
We started with 2 cups of flour,
a cup of sugar, a teaspoon of baking powder.

Sanity

Rising to greet you.
Pulling out a chair.
Licking your plate clean.

Sanity bread crumbs sticking to the side of
your mouth your chin my shirt until
wiped away soft backhand skin.

Sanity letting you sit down first.

Beached and bleached into blue-white seashell fragments.
Crushed and sprinkled over a wide path.

Then sanity taking a nap.

In Florida

In Florida, the land of the dead for me.
All those memories bouncing on
  airboats through swamps
  wandering around exotic bird parks,
  listening to King Crimson
    on the wide lawn
    under the wide sky
    by the reflecting lagoon.

Walking over to my great aunts' and uncles' apartments
for bowl snacks and conversation.
There was that one time—
  Meyer borrowed our walkman.
  Volume spun all the way up,
  all the way up
    he could hear again.
And oh my god such a smile.

All gone now, that gang.
  There were *two* Irvings.

All alligators gone.
All tennis courts gone.
All rec centers gone
  with miles of immaculate green felt pool tables.

Key West too.

And Florida is for me.
The land of the dead for me.

Smaller, Slender, Grave

Other people have smaller fingers
slender, grave pincers
and they move fragments around.
The smallest
reposition dust to achieve a fine result.

Not children. I'm not
talking about children
or woodland creatures.

Other grown-ups.
Living in crash pads
with thatched chairs and
acoustic proto-guitars
hung by the door.

Look at them. Look
at their work.

Shaved My Beard

I shaved my beard today so, hopefully, we can put our feud aside.
You thought I was making fun of the '70s, but I wasn't.
I love the '70s.
That's why I wore the beard in the first place. Can't you understand?

It was starting to tear the block apart, our feud.
People were taking sides. Mostly they were taking your side.
And that made me angry.

So I yelled at your cat. So I took your mailbox.
So I rubbed my butt on your car. So what, right?
Really. I mean, we're grown-ups, you and I.
Look: I shaved my beard.

Let's get on with our lives.

No One Should Suffer

Some say "no one should suffer simply because
they have chosen to
fall in love."
But I'm not certain I agree.

Surely someone should suffer.
Surely. Someone should suffer simply.
Because they have
chosen to fall.

You think?
But perhaps no one have chosen?

I'm say not certain.
Surely to choose to love, yes?

Surely to choose perhaps
to love at last
to fall
simply because

but no one agree.

The Pencil They Gave Me

The pencil they gave me
was covered with paint. I scraped at it

artisan, whole-leaf paint chips
dropped off
in spidery clumps.

And now I can see, it is an artisan pencil.
Made by a man from the mountains of Peru.
And there's my friend, the legendary artisan

with his Peruvian pencil-carving knife gripped, its handle
snapped clean
from the root of some
mountain vegetable.

Most of the knife is edible, in fact.
Even the blade if you cook it long enough.

But who would eat such a thing?
Who would eat the knife cooked
calm til fiber rests, naps, curled?

Someone with a pen, no doubt. Or a typewriter.

Soul

Soul is not space,
not molecules.

You can fit all the world's souls
in the crack
of your ass.

However,

just because you *can*
doesn't mean you *should*.

Espresso Poems

I write espresso poems now
the way I used to write about cigarettes.
My old fumbled word love to white ash
the hard-dented tan filter.
The clouds! Oh those sainted particles!
The courage of my glass ashtray!
All swapped for

a slight-stained saucer
a cup
a cat-like crema.

How long till they turn you against me?
What will I smoke when you're gone?

The Perfect Gentleman

At an Italian restaurant last night, while I was picking at my spaghetti bolognese, a perfect little gentleman of around two or three years old came up to me and stared.

Whatever I did—peekaboo, wiggly fingers, wiggly fingers on head, big smile, surprise face—it didn't matter. He just stared. It was wonderful.

And once again I found myself so grateful that I don't live in Belgium or Austria or one of those other places (Portugal) where they take their children and send them into the forest and don't let them come back until they're twenty-five.

You can criticize Americans and say that we watch too much TV or that we put feathers in places we probably shouldn't (egg dishes), but you have to admit: at least we don't make our young people live in the forest.

www.ingramcontent.com/pod-product-compliance
Lightning Source LLC
Chambersburg PA
CBHW030159100526
44592CB00009B/350